DANIIL KARABUT

Rise to Greatness

Harnessing the Power of Positive Thinking and Action

Contents

I

Introduction

Introduction

Have you ever felt stuck in a rut, struggling to find motivation and purpose in life? Have you found yourself constantly dwelling on negative thoughts and experiences, unable to break free from their grip? If so, you are not alone. Many of us struggle with negativity and a lack of direction at some point. However, the good news is that there is a solution: harnessing the power of positive thinking and action.

In this book, "Rise to Greatness: Harnessing the Power of Positive Thinking and Action," you will learn the importance of positive thinking and how it can impact every aspect of your life. We will explore techniques for developing a positive mindset, taking positive action, and integrating these practices into your daily life. You will discover the benefits of a positive lifestyle, including increased happiness, better relationships, and improved health.

Through practical advice and real-life examples, this book will provide the tools and inspiration you need to break free from negative thinking and achieve greatness. Whether you want to improve your personal or professional life, this book will guide you on a journey of growth and transformation. So, are you ready to embrace the power of positive thinking and action and rise to greatness? Let's get started.

II

Part 1

Understanding the Power of Positive Thinking

This section will delve into positive thinking and its impact on our lives. We will start by defining positive thinking and explaining its benefits.

Definition of Positive Thinking: Positive thinking is a mental and emotional attitude that focuses on the good in people, situations, and outcomes. It involves looking for the silver lining in every situation and maintaining a hopeful outlook, even in adversity.

Benefits of Positive Thinking: Positive thinking has been shown to have a range of benefits, including increased happiness, better health, improved relationships, and enhanced performance in both personal and professional settings. When we adopt a positive mindset, we are more likely to approach challenges with a solution-focused attitude rather than becoming bogged down by negativity and stress.

The Role of Positive Thinking in Personal and Professional Growth: Positive thinking is essential to personal and professional growth. It helps us to set and achieve our goals, maintain healthy relationships, and develop a sense of fulfillment and purpose. A positive attitude can lead to increased productivity, better teamwork, and improved job satisfaction in the workplace.

Common Misconceptions and Challenges of Positive Thinking: While positive thinking is widely recognized as a valuable tool for personal and professional development, there are also misconceptions and challenges associated with this approach. Some believe positive thinking means ignoring or denying negative experiences and emotions. Others may struggle to maintain a positive outlook in adversity or hardship.

This section will address these misconceptions and challenges and provide strategies for overcoming them. By the end of this section, you will deeply understand the power of positive thinking and how it can impact your life.

However, it's important to note that positive thinking does not mean ignoring or denying negative experiences and emotions. Instead, it means approaching these experiences with a solution-focused attitude, seeking to understand and learn from them, and looking for the good they can bring. Positive thinking also involves being mindful of our thoughts and emotions and consciously focusing on the positive aspects of our lives and experiences.

One of the challenges of positive thinking is maintaining a positive outlook in the face of adversity or hardship. It can be difficult to remain optimistic when faced with setbacks, failures, or adverse circumstances. However, it's precisely in these moments that positive thinking can be most beneficial. By adopting a positive mindset, we can turn challenges into opportunities for growth and improvement and find the strength to keep moving forward.

In conclusion, positive thinking is a powerful tool for personal and professional growth but requires effort and practice. By developing a positive mindset, taking positive action, and integrating these practices into our daily lives, we can harness the power of positive thinking and achieve greatness. In the following sections, we will explore techniques and strategies for developing a positive mindset and taking positive action so that you can start experiencing the benefits of positive thinking for yourself.

III

Part 2

Developing a Positive Mindset

This section will focus on developing a positive mindset, which is the foundation for harnessing the power of positive thinking and action. A positive attitude involves cultivating an optimistic outlook and focusing on the good in people, situations, and outcomes.

Techniques for Cultivating a Positive Mindset: Several methods can be used to cultivate a positive mindset, including:

1. Gratitude: Practicing gratitude involves focusing on the things in our lives that we are thankful for and expressing appreciation for them. This can help to shift our focus from negative experiences and emotions to positive ones.
2. Visualization: Visualization involves creating a mental image of a desired outcome or experience and focusing on this image regularly. This can help us to remain motivated and optimistic, even in the face of challenges.
3. Reframing Negative Thoughts: Reframing negative thoughts involves changing how we think about negative experiences and looking for the good that can come from them. This can help us to maintain a positive outlook, even in difficult circumstances.

The Importance of Self-Awareness and Self-Reflection: Developing a positive mindset involves self-awareness and self-reflection. By becoming more aware of our thoughts and emotions and how they impact our experiences, we can consciously focus on the positive aspects of our lives.

Maintaining a Positive Outlook in Challenging Situations: While it's important to cultivate a positive mindset, it's also essential to maintain a positive outlook in challenging situations. This can involve seeking support from friends, family, or a mental health professional, practicing self-care, and finding healthy ways to cope with stress and negativity.

This section will explore these techniques and strategies in more detail and provide practical advice for developing and maintaining a positive mindset. By the end of this section, you will have the tools you need to cultivate a positive outlook and approach life with a solution-focused attitude.

It's important to remember that developing a positive mindset takes time and effort. It's not a one-time event but a continuous self-reflection, learning, and growth process. However, the benefits of a positive mindset are well worth the effort. By cultivating an optimistic outlook, we can improve our personal and professional relationships, enhance our performance, and increase our happiness and well-being.

This section explored the importance of developing a positive mindset and provided techniques and strategies for cultivating a positive outlook. By consciously focusing on the good in people, situations, and outcomes, we can create a foundation for positive thinking and action and achieve greatness in our lives. The following section will explore how to take positive action and turn our positive mindset into positive results.

IV

Part 3

Taking Positive Action

In this section, we will focus on taking positive action, which is the next step in harnessing the power of positive thinking. Positive action involves turning our positive mindset into concrete results and achieving our goals.

The Connection between Positive Thinking and Action: Positive thinking and action are interconnected. When we adopt a positive mindset, we approach challenges with a solution-focused attitude and are more likely to take positive action. On the other hand, taking positive action can reinforce our positive mindset and lead to tremendous success and fulfillment.

Setting Clear and Achievable Goals: Setting clear and achievable goals is essential to taking positive action. This involves defining what we want to achieve, breaking down our goals into smaller, manageable steps, and setting deadlines for completion.

Taking Positive Action and Overcoming Obstacles: Positive action also involves overcoming obstacles and setbacks. This can include seeking support from others, developing a growth mindset, and finding creative solutions to problems. It's important to remember that obstacles and failures are a normal part of the journey toward success and can provide valuable opportunities for learning and growth.

This section will explore these concepts in more detail and provide practical advice for taking positive action and achieving our goals. By the end of this section, you will have the tools and inspiration to turn your positive mindset into positive results and achieve greatness in your life.

It's also important to note that taking positive action requires discipline and perseverance. Positive thinking alone is not enough to achieve our goals. We need to take consistent, deliberate steps toward our objectives and be willing to put in the effort required to succeed.

One way to maintain momentum and stay motivated is to celebrate your progress and successes. It's important to acknowledge and appreciate the small and big wins, as they prove your progress and give you the confidence to keep moving forward.

Another critical factor in taking positive action is maintaining a growth mindset. A growth mindset involves seeing challenges and failures as opportunities for growth and learning rather than setbacks or defeats. Adopting a growth mindset makes us more likely to persevere in adversity and find creative solutions to problems.

In conclusion, taking positive action is essential to harnessing the power of positive thinking. By setting clear and achievable goals, taking consistent and deliberate steps towards our objectives, and maintaining a growth mindset, we can turn our positive attitude into positive results and achieve greatness in our lives. In the final section, we will explore how to integrate positive thinking and action into our daily lives and live a positive and fulfilling life.

V

Part 4

Living a Positive Life

This section will explore how to integrate positive thinking and action into our daily lives and live a positive and fulfilling life.

Integrating Positive Thinking and Action into Daily Life: Integrating positive thinking and action into daily life involves making these practices a habit and incorporating them into our routines and behaviors. This can include setting aside time each day for self-reflection and gratitude, practicing visualization, and consciously focusing on the positive aspects of our experiences.

The Benefits of a Positive Lifestyle: Living a joyous life has many benefits, including increased happiness, better relationships, and improved health. When we adopt a positive outlook, we are more likely to approach challenges with a solution-focused attitude and find joy and fulfillment in our daily lives.

Creating and Maintaining a Positive and Fulfilling Life: Creating and maintaining a positive and fulfilling life involves setting and achieving our goals, developing and maintaining positive relationships, and engaging in activities and experiences that bring us joy and fulfillment. It also consists in caring for our physical, emotional, and mental well-being and seeking support and guidance when needed.

This section will explore these concepts in more detail and

provide practical advice for creating and maintaining a positive and fulfilling life. By the end of this section, you will have the tools and inspiration you need to live a positive and fulfilling life and achieve greatness in all aspects.

It's important to remember that positive life is not about perfection but progress. There will be ups and downs along the way and challenges and obstacles. However, by maintaining a positive outlook, taking positive action, and seeking support and guidance, we can navigate these challenges and continue to grow and evolve.

Another critical aspect of living a positive life is cultivating a sense of purpose and meaning. This can involve finding activities and experiences that align with our values and passions and using our skills and abilities to impact the world positively. When we have a sense of purpose and meaning, we are more likely to experience a sense of fulfillment and satisfaction and to approach life with an optimistic outlook.

In conclusion, living a positive life is about integrating positive thinking and action into our daily lives and seeking joy, fulfillment, and purpose in all our lives. By consciously focusing on the positive and approaching challenges with a solution-focused attitude, we can live a positive and fulfilling life and achieve greatness in all our lives.

VI

Conclusion

Conclusion

In this book, we have explored the power of positive thinking and action and the impact these practices can have on our lives. We have covered the importance of developing a positive mindset, taking positive action, and living a positive and fulfilling life. Through practical advice and real-life examples, we have provided the tools and inspiration you need to harness the power of positive thinking and achieve greatness in your life.

Recap of Key Points: In this book, we have discussed the following key points:

The definition of positive thinking and its benefits.

Techniques for developing a positive mindset include gratitude, visualization, and reframing negative thoughts.

The connection between positive thinking and action and the importance of setting clear and achievable goals.

The benefits of living a positive life and how to integrate positive thinking and move into daily life.

Encouragement to Embrace Positive Thinking and Action: We encourage you to embrace positive thinking and action in your own life and start experiencing the benefits of these practices. Whether you want to improve your personal or professional life or achieve greatness in all aspects of your life, positive thinking and action are powerful tools for growth and transformation.

Final Thoughts and Inspiration for Continued Growth and Success: We hope this book has provided you with the inspiration and guidance you need to harness the power of positive thinking and action and achieve greatness in your life. Remember that the journey toward positive thought and action is a continuous process of self-reflection, learning, and growth. So, keep moving forward, embrace positive thinking and effort, and rise to greatness.